In Search of
GREAT WHITE SHARKS

Martin Chilson

PowerKiDS press™

New York

Published in 2016 by The Rosen Publishing Group, Inc.
29 East 21st Street, New York, NY 10010

First Edition

Editor: Caitie McAneney
Book Design: Mickey Harmon

Photo Credits: Cover (iron bars) Wayne Lynch/All Canada Photos/Getty Images; cover, pp. 1, 3, 4, 6, 8, 10, 12, 14, 16, 18, 20–24 (background) Ase/Shutterstock.com; cover (great white shark) Stefan Pircher/Shutterstock.com; pp. 5, 22 nitrogenic.com/Shutterstock.com; p. 7 Fiona Ayerst/Shutterstock.com; p. 9 (main) Elsa Hoffmann/Shutterstock.com; p. 9 (inset) Roger de la Harpe/Gallo Images/Getty Images; p. 11 Jim Agronick/Shutterstock.com; p. 13 Educational Images/Contributor/Universal Images Group/Getty Images; p. 14 mingis/Shutterstock.com; pp. 15, 17 (main), 20 Sergey Uryadinakov/Shutterstock.com; p. 17 (inset) RAEVSKY/Shutterstock.com; p. 19 Per-Gunnar Ostby/Oxford Scientific/Getty Images.

Library of Congress Cataloging-in-Publication Data

Chilson, Martin, author.
 In search of Great White sharks / Martin Chilson.
     pages cm. — (Shark search)
 Includes index.
 ISBN 978-1-5081-4339-0 (pbk.)
 ISBN 978-1-5081-4340-6 (6 pack)
 ISBN 978-1-5081-4341-3 (library binding)
 1. White shark—Juvenile literature. 2. White shark—Behavior—Juvenile literature. I. Title.
 QL638.95L3 C55 2016
 597.3'3—dc23
                         2015023512

Manufactured in the United States of America

CPSIA Compliance Information: Batch #BW16PK: For Further Information contact Rosen Publishing, New York, New York at 1-800-237-9932

Contents

Great White Up Close. 4

Beastly Bodies. 6

Terrific Teeth 8

Supersenses 10

Raising Their Young. 12

What Do Great Whites Eat? 14

A Hunter's Habitat. 16

Helpful Hunters 18

Watch Out! 20

Saving the Great White 22

Glossary 23

Index 24

Websites 24

Great White Up Close

Imagine you're swimming in the ocean. You see a huge shark with a white underside. That shark is one of the deadliest hunters in the world—the great white!

As the shark swims toward you, you see a pointed **snout** and many sharp teeth. A great white's **skeleton** is made of cartilage, which is the same bendable matter that makes up your nose and ears. This special, bendable skeleton lets the shark move smoothly and quickly through the water. Read on to find out more about the great white shark!

Adult great white sharks are usually around 15 feet (4.6 m) long, but can grow to be more than 20 feet (6.1 m) long! They can weigh more than 5,000 pounds (2,268 kg).

5

Beastly Bodies

Is a great white shark actually white? Only the underside of a great white shark is white. The rest of the shark is bluish gray to grayish brown.

Sharks are fish, so they have fins to help them swim. They also have **gills** to breathe. However, sharks have scales that are different from most fish. Shark skin looks smooth, but it's actually rough. It's covered with flat, tooth-like scales. The scales move smoothly through water, allowing sharks to swim very quickly and quietly.

The great white shark has been around for millions of years. That's because its body is perfectly matched to its **habitat**.

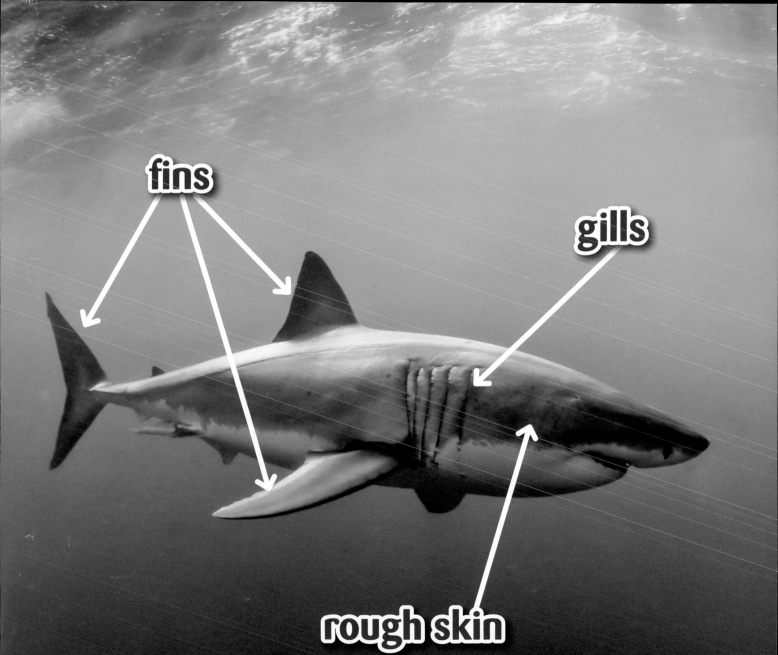

Terrific Teeth

If you're a fish, the last place you want to end up is in a shark's mouth. The great white shark's mouth is huge. It can be 39 inches (1 m) across, and it's full of knife-sharp teeth. These teeth can be up to 3 inches (8 cm) long!

Each tooth has a sawlike edge. This allows the shark to easily cut through meat. A great white can have up to 300 teeth arranged in several rows.

A great white shark's jaws are so powerful, and its teeth so sharp, it can bite right through its **prey**!

great white shark's jaw

Supersenses

Over time, the great white shark **developed** supersenses to help it live and hunt in the water. The great white shark has outstanding eyesight, which helps it spot prey. This shark also has a strong sense of smell, which is stronger than that of any other shark. It can smell just one drop of blood in 10 billion drops of water!

Perhaps the great white shark's most **amazing** sense is its sense of touch. It can feel very small movements in the water.

Sharks can even sense electric fields. This helps them **navigate** through the water and find prey.

Raising Their Young

You may not believe it, but each huge great white shark starts out as just a tiny egg. Female great whites can carry up to 10 eggs inside their body for a year or more. Unlike most fish, a great white mother gives birth to live babies. Baby sharks are called pups.

A pup can be almost 5 feet (1.5 m) long when it's born! From the moment it's born, the pup is on its own. The mother leaves the pup and swims away.

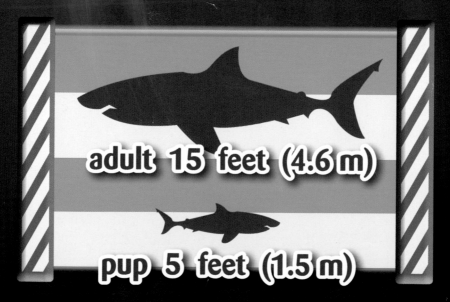

adult 15 feet (4.6 m)

pup 5 feet (1.5 m)

When a pup is born, it already has sharp teeth.
It's ready to hunt!

What Do Great Whites Eat?

The great white shark is at the top of its **food chain**. That means that it doesn't have any natural predators and has plenty of natural prey. In fact, the great white shark will eat almost anything!

A great white's favorite foods are seals, sea lions, elephant seals, dolphins, and walruses. They like to eat these animals because they're high in fat. That gives the great white the power it needs to swim and hunt.

SHARK SIGHTED TODAY

ENTER WATER AT OWN RISK

If you're swimming in a great white habitat, watch out. Unlike some other sharks, great whites hunt during the daytime. They don't want to eat you, but there's a chance they'll take a bite!

15

A Hunter's Habitat

Where does the great white shark make its home? It spends much of its time swimming along the coasts of most **continents**. It favors places where the water is not too hot or too cold.

Great whites are found in the waters around North America, Australia, Japan, the northern coast of Africa, and in the Mediterranean Sea, among other places. They follow their food, often moving around in search of their next meal. They like to swim around small islands because sea lions and seals live there.

Great white sharks hunt near coasts because that's where seals and sea lions like to live.

great white shark range

Helpful Hunters

Great white sharks play an important part in keeping the ocean healthy. How do these scary sharks help their habitat? They feed on hurt and dead animals. They also keep the numbers of fish and other animals from becoming too great.

While killer whales and other sharks sometimes kill great whites, they're usually left alone. The greatest risk comes from people. People kill great white sharks for their skin, meat, liver, jaw, and fins.

Some sharks get caught in fishing nets when they go after a fish.

19

Watch Out!

There's probably no other ocean animal that's as scary as the great white shark. But the truth is, this shark isn't looking to eat people.

Many believe great white attacks on people are just a mistake. People often surf and swim in a shark's hunting grounds. Sharks hunt from underneath their prey, and a person's outline might look like a seal or dolphin. You might think great white sharks attack people all the time. In reality, there are fewer than 100 shark attacks on people each year, and only around five are **fatal**.

Shark Bites!

 Great white sharks can live up to 60 years.

 A great white shark can **breach** out of the water like a whale.

 A great white can swim about 15 miles (24 km) per hour. That's fast!

 A great white shark can sense small amounts of blood up to three miles (4.8 km) away.

 The great white shark has taste buds inside its throat and mouth so it knows what it's about to swallow.

 One great white shark was tracked as it swam from South Africa to Australia in the longest recorded journey of any fish.

Saving the Great White

Great whites are one of the 64 shark species, or kinds, that are endangered. Endangered animals are at risk of dying out. The great white's population is decreasing because people catch and kill too many.

You might not think a huge hunter like the great white needs **protection**. However, it can take a long time for the number of sharks to grow. How can you help?

Teach others about this amazing creature. After all, it would rather swim the seas freely than bite a person any day!

Glossary

amazing: Causing great surprise or wonder.

breach: To leap out of the water.

continent: One of Earth's seven great landmasses.

develop: To grow and change over time.

fatal: Causing death.

food chain: A line of living things, each of which uses the one before it for food.

gill: The body part that ocean animals such as fish use to breathe in water.

habitat: The natural home for plants, animals, and other living things.

navigate: To find one's way.

prey: An animal hunted by other animals for food.

protection: The act of keeping something or someone safe.

skeleton: The strong frame that supports an animal's body.

snout: An animal's nose and mouth.

Index

A
attacks, 20

B
babies, 12

C
coasts, 16

E
eggs, 12
electric fields, 10
endangered, 22
eyesight, 10

F
fins, 6, 7, 18
food chain, 14
foods, 14, 16

G
gills, 6, 7

H
habitat, 6, 15,
    16, 18

J
jaws, 8, 9, 18

P
people, 18, 20, 22
prey, 8, 10, 14, 20
protection, 22
pups, 12, 13

S
sense of smell,
    10
sense of touch,
    10
skeleton, 4
snout, 4

T
teeth, 4, 8, 13

Websites

Due to the changing nature of Internet links, PowerKids Press has developed an online list of websites related to the subject of this book. This site is updated regularly. Please use this link to access the list: www.powerkidslinks.com/search/great